Do-It-Yourself Wedding Ceremony Guidebook

Choosing the Perfect Words and Officiating Your Unforgettable Day

Dayna Reid

Printed in the United States of America
First Printing: May 2014

International Standard Book Number-13: 978-1499204216 (Softcover)
International Standard Book Number-10: 1499204213 (Softcover)

Visit the author's website at www.DaynaReid.com
Visit the book website at www.Marriage-Vows.com

Dedication

I am so very grateful and appreciative of my daughter Shayla and my son Delane. While they are vastly different in their outlooks and roads chosen in life, each one's unique strength of character, values, and love have consistently supported and encouraged me on my own life path. They continuously remind me of what is possible when you are deeply loved.

Contents

Introduction

Did you know that you can fully customize not only the vows, but *all* the words spoken during your ceremony? When planning a wedding, there are many resources available to assist you with all the details to make it a *visual* dream, but what about the ceremony itself? Wouldn't you like the same attention to detail and extensive variety of personalized choices for the most important aspect of your wedding—the *words* spoken to seal your commitment to each other?

Within these pages you will find everything you need to easily create and conduct a ceremony that genuinely expresses to your guests what your beliefs are about the significance of marriage and accurately communicates the true intentions of the promises you wish to make to each other.

Who should read this book?

This book provides you (the couple getting married or renewing their vows) as well as officiants or ministers with all the information needed to compose and carry out a truly meaningful wedding ceremony, including information on selecting an Officiant (or becoming ordained if you wish to have a friend or family member officiate the ceremony or wish to officiate weddings as a business), obtaining the marriage license and filing the paperwork.

How to use this book

You may choose to start with learning all about "Making It Legal," or you may choose to go directly to the "Wedding Ceremony Elements Overview" section which describes the traditional wedding ceremony elements and the meaning behind each one, aiding you in deciding what to include and what to leave out of your ceremony.

To compliment the traditional elements, you may wish to include additional touches, such as a Candle Lighting Ceremony, Rose Ceremony, remembering loved ones unable to attend or including children.

Once you have selected the elements that are important to you, you may begin your search for the words to express your personal thoughts and beliefs for each element. There are many resources available for finding the best wording for each element.

My book "Sacred Ceremony: Create and Officiate Personalized Wedding Ceremonies" has a variety of spiritual and non-spiritual wording selections and additional alternatives to choose from for every element of the ceremony. There are also other books, as well as many online resources.

Sample ceremonies (including vow renewal ceremonies) are provided in this book. You may choose one of the samples for your wedding, or simply as a starting point to generate ideas for composing your ceremony. Note: All wording can be easily altered for use in a Renewal of Vows ceremony.

Now let's begin the journey of designing the ceremony that expresses your deepest desire for each other and your marriage....

Wedding Ceremony Elements Overview

There are many elements to choose from when creating your ceremony, but there are only two elements that are legally required; the Declaration of Intent and the Pronouncement of marriage. In other words, you could literally have a ceremony that read: "Jane, do you agree to marry Joe? And Joe, do you agree to marry Jane? I now pronounce you married." All other elements are optional, which gives you tremendous flexibility in designing a ceremony that is the most meaningful to the two of you.

In addition to the basic elements of a traditional ceremony, there are many other special touches that can be added to your ceremony to make it unique and your own, such as including children, honoring parents or grandparents, remembering loved ones that are unable to attend or have passed on, etc. (the book "Sacred Ceremony: Create and Officiate Personalized Wedding

Ceremonies" includes these and many other ideas on customizing your Wedding).

Traditional Ceremony Elements and Their Purposes

As you read through the description for each of the traditional ceremony elements in this section, you may choose which elements to include and which ones to leave out of your ceremony.

Procession

(also known as the Wedding March)

This is the choreographed walk down the aisle of the wedding party to the altar. This symbolically represents two things: the couple's transition from their individual lives to the union of marriage and the wedding attendants' support of the union by taking part in the same walk.

The Officiant, Groom and Best Man wait at the altar for the wedding party to walk down the aisle in the following order; first the Groomsmen paired with the Bridesmaids, followed by the Maid or Matron of Honor, then the Ring Bearer, then the Flower Girl, and lastly the Bride and her Father. Facing the altar, the women will be on the left and the men will be on the right.

In addition, traditionally, the guests will be seated on the same side of the altar as the one (bride or groom) who invited them. But a more contemporary arrangement for the guests is to be seated on the opposite side as the one who invited them so that their guests may see their face during the ceremony instead of their back.

Music played for the Procession can be a single selection or multiple selections (a selection for the wedding party and a different selection for the Bride, etc).

Order of Procession

(Keep in mind that it is your wedding and you may arrange your wedding party in any order you choose.)

Officiant/Minister ☐ ◯ **Groom**
◯ Best Man
Bridesmaid ◯ ◯ Groomsman
Bridesmaid ◯ ◯ Groomsman
Bridesmaid ◯ ◯ Groomsman
◯ Maid/Matron of Honor
◯ Ring Bearer
◯ Flower Girl
Bride ◯ ◯ Bride's Father

Order at the Altar

(Keep in mind that it is your wedding and you may arrange your wedding party in any order you choose.)

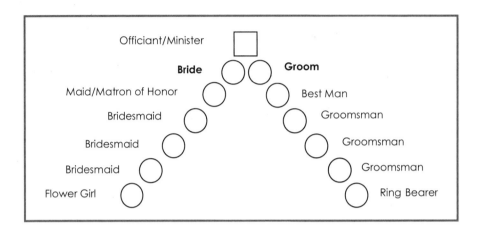

Approval Blessing

(Also known as the "Give Away")

This element gives others the opportunity to give their approval or blessing on the ceremony that is about to take place. Traditionally the father or the parents of the Bride answer "I do" or "We do" to a question asked by the Officiant.

Welcome/Introduction

(Also known as the Convocation)

This element calls together all in attendance to begin the ceremony. The words spoken at this time welcome and thank the guests as well as introduce the purpose of this gathering.

Opening Blessing

(a prayer also known as the Invocation)

The words spoken at this time are intended to invoke a higher source (God, Goddess, Great Spirit, the Universe, etc) to elevate the intent of the ceremony.

The Address

(also known as the Sermon)

This element shares with the guests, the couple's beliefs on the meaning of marriage, and is designed to encourage reflection on the significance of this commitment. This may also include a historical reflection on the couple's relationship up until this point, as well as the story of how the couple met.

Dedication Blessing

(a prayer also known as the Consecration)

The words spoken at this time are meant to elevate the intent of the message communicated in the Address and remind everyone that the commitment about to be made is sacred.

This element also provides a transition from the message about marriage just spoken to the actual promises that the couple is about to make to seal their commitment.

Declaration of Intent

(a legally required element of the ceremony)

This element is the "I Do" section of the ceremony. The words spoken at this time declare the couple's intention to marry.

The declaration is customarily made by the Bride and Groom each answering, "I do" or "I will" in response to a question presented by the Officiant.

The Vows

This element is the verbal exchange between the couple that expresses the sincere promises they are making to each other regarding their intention for the marriage.

The words spoken at this time may be memorized, read from paper, or recited after the Officiant.

Ring Blessing

The words spoken at this time describe the purpose of exchanging the rings and the sentiment that the couple wishes to be reminded of as they wear them.

Exchanging of the Rings

This element is the physical exchange of wedding rings and the verbal exchange between the couple that expresses the significance of this offering. The words spoken at this time may be memorized, read from paper, or recited after the Officiant.

Pronouncement of Marriage
(a legally required element of the ceremony)

This element is the pronouncement that the couple is officially wed.

The Kiss

This element is a kiss shared between the couple and symbolically represents the sealing of the promises made. The words spoken at this time instruct the couple to kiss.

Closing Blessing

(a prayer also known as the Benediction)

The words spoken at this time are meant to send the couple off into their new future together, and to communicate the hopes and wishes for that future.

The Presentation

This element is the official introduction of the newly married couple.

The Recession

This element is the choreographed walk down the aisle of the wedding party away from the altar and to the festivities. This walk signifies the completion of the ceremony and the beginning of the celebration. Traditionally, the wedding party exits in the opposite order they entered with the Bride and Groom exiting first.

Order of Recession

(Keep in mind that it is your wedding and you may arrange your wedding party in any order you choose.)

Readings and Additional Ceremony Elements

Readings consist of one or more selections (poems, lyrics, stories, etc.) to be read aloud during carefully selected moments throughout the ceremony. The selections are meant to convey a feeling or message that provides a window into the couple's unique world and may be read by a friend, family member or the Officiant. Readings may also be incorporated into the ceremony as the wording for one of the traditional ceremony elements.

Additional Ceremony Elements are special purpose mini ceremonies that are performed to further symbolically demonstrate any commitments or statements you wish to communicate. For example, a Candle Lighting Ceremony (the lighting of a single unity candle, by the bride and groom with individual taper candles) may be included to symbolize the joining together of two lives into one.

Sample Ceremonies

Welcome

We have come here today, to celebrate and support the choice of (*Person A's name*) and (*Person B's name*) to join in marriage. Love is a miraculous gift, and a wedding is a celebration of that magic, and that's why we are here today, to share in that magic!

Declaration of Intent

(*Person A's name*), Do you take (*Person B's name*) to be your (husband/wife), to love, honor, comfort and cherish, from this day forward?

(Person A answers: 'I Do')

(*Person B's name*), Do you take (*Person A's name*) to be your (wife/husband), to love, honor, comfort and cherish, from this day forward?

(Person B answers: 'I Do')

Ring Exchange

And now, seal your promises with these rings, the symbol of the life you share together.

(Person A's name), repeat after me;

> *(Person B's name),* this ring is a symbol, of my promise, to always be, your lover, companion, and friend.

(Person B's name), repeat after me;

> *(Person A's name),* this ring is a symbol, of my promise, to always be, your lover, companion, and friend.

Pronouncement of Marriage

Now, because you have chosen one another, and vowed to love each other in marriage, it gives me great joy to pronounce you (husband and wife/married).

You may kiss.

I introduce to you, (*Person A's name*) and (*Person B's name*) (*last name*).

Traditional (Spiritual) Ceremony

Approval Blessing
(*To Person B's Father, or other special people giving blessing, or all people in attendance*)

> Who gives their blessing on this union between (*Person B's name*) and (*Person A's name*)?

(*Response*) (<u>I do/We do</u>).

Welcome/Introduction

(*Person B's name*) and (*Person A's name*), today you are surrounded by your family and friends. All of whom are gathered to witness your exchange of vows and to share in the joy of this occasion. Let this be a statement of what you mean to each other, and the commitment of marriage that you will make.

Address

As you know, no one person can marry you. Only you can marry yourselves. By a mutual commitment to love each other, to work toward creating an atmosphere of care, consideration and respect, by a willingness to face life's anxieties together, you can make your wedded life your strength.

On this day of your wedding you stand somewhat apart from other people. You stand within the light of your love; and this is as it should be. You will experience a lot together, some wonderful, some difficult. But even when it is difficult you must manage to call upon the strength in the love you have for each other to see you through. From this day onward you must come closer together than ever before, you must love one another with the strength that makes this bond a marriage. As you exchange your vows, remember that the sensual part of love is great, but when this is combined with real friendship both are infinitely enhanced.

Dedication Blessing

I would like at this time to speak of some things, which we pray for you. First, we pray for you a love that continues to give you joy and peace that provides you with energy to face the responsibilities of life. We pray for you a home of serenity. Not just a place of private joy and retreat, but a temple wherein the values of God and family are generated and upheld. Finally, we pray that as you grow together, you are able to look back at your lives together, and say these two things to each other: Because you loved me, you have given me faith in myself; because I have seen the good in you, I have received from you a faith in humanity.

Declaration of Intent

(To Person A)

(*Person A's name*), Do you promise (*Person B's name*), that from this day onward you will stand with (him/her) in sickness and health, in joy and sorrow, and do you pledge to (him/her) your respect and your love?
> *(Person A) I do.*

(To Person B)

(*Person B's name*), Do you promise (*Person A's name*), that from this day onward you will stand with (him/her) in sickness and health, in joy and sorrow, and do you pledge to (him/her) your respect and your love?

> *(Person B) I do.*

Reading

(A special selection of your choice.)

Vows

<u>*(Person A's name)*</u>, repeat after me.

> (Person B's name), today we begin our lives together.
> I promise before God, our families and our friends
> to be your faithful (husband/wife).
> I choose to live with you, as your lover, companion and friend,
> loving you when life is peaceful, and when it is painful,
> during our successes, and during our failures,
> supported by your strengths,
> and accepting your weaknesses.
> I will honor your goals and dreams,
> trying always, to encourage your fulfillment.
> I will strive to be honest, and open with you,
> sharing my thoughts, and my life with you.
> I promise to love and cherish you
> from this day forward.

<u>*(Person B's name)*</u>, repeat after me.

> (Person A's name), today we begin our lives together.
> I promise before God, our families and our friends
> to be your faithful (wife/husband).

I choose to live with you, as your lover, companion and friend,
loving you when life is peaceful, and when it is painful,
during our successes, and during our failures,
supported by your strengths,
and accepting your weaknesses.
I will honor your goals and dreams,
trying always, to encourage your fulfillment.
I will strive to be honest, and open with you,
sharing my thoughts, and my life with you.
I promise to love and cherish you
from this day forward.

Ring Blessing

These rings are an outward and visible sign of an inward and spiritual grace. Signifying to all the uniting of (_Person B's name_) and (_Person A's name_) in the bond of matrimony. In the presence of God and these friends, seal your promises with rings, the symbol of the life you share together.

Exchanging of the Rings

(_Person A's name_), repeat after me.

(_Person B's name_), In token and pledge, of the vow made between us, with this ring, I thee wed.

(_Person B's name_), repeat after me.

(_Person A's name_), In token and pledge, of the vow made between us, with this ring, I thee wed.

Prayer

(A prayer selection of your choice, or have a friend or family member say one.)

Candle Lighting Ceremony

(The couple light a Unity candle with tapers that are already lit.)

Pronouncement of Marriage

(*Person B's name*) and (*Person A's name*) on behalf of all those present, and by the strength of your own love, I pronounce you married, and may the blessing of God be with you.

You may kiss.

I introduce to you (*Person B's name*) and (*Person A's name*) (last name), married.

Contemporary (Non-spiritual) Ceremony

Welcome/Introduction

(_Person B's name_) and (_Person A's name_) have invited you here today to share with them in this joyous celebration of their love and desire to join their lives together in marriage. We are here to rejoice and remember that it is love that leads us to our true destinations and to celebrate with (_Person B's name_) and (_Person A's name_) on their arrival in love and respect at this altar.

We are here to celebrate the marriage of (_Person B's name_) and (_Person A's name_), to honor the beginning of their new life.

We're here to listen, to love, to dance and celebrate, and to send them into their future with our outrageous, loving, support. So sit back now, open your hearts, and let the wedding begin!

Opening Blessing

Marriage is a very special place, the sheltered environment in which we can endlessly explore ourselves in the presence of another and in which we can offer the possibility of true reflection of another. May the vision that (_Person B's name_) and (_Person A's name_) have of one another be always informed by the radiant force that first brought them together, and we wish that as they move into the sanctity of marriage that they always hold one another in the love of all love.

Candles for Parents

Marriage is a venture of faith. It is a life of loving, comforting, honoring and keeping. (_Person B's name_) and (_Person A's_ _name_) bring to this venture their unique history and personality. Part of their history was shared with their loved ones who have passed on. In memory of their lives, they light these candles in our midst, in celebration of this marriage.

[Person A lights candle]　　　　(_Person A's name_), will now light a candle,

　　　　in memory of (_names of loved ones to be remembered_).

[Person B lights candle]　　　　(_Person B's name_), will now light a candle,

　　　　in memory of (_names of loved ones to be remembered_).

Reading
And now (_Friend's name_) will read a selection chosen by (_Person B's name_) and (_Person A's name_).

　　　　(A special selection of your choice.)

Song
And now (_Friend's name_) will (sing/perform) a song chosen by (_Person B's name_) and (_Person A's name_).

　　　　(A special selection of your choice.)

Address

Marriage symbolizes the ultimate intimacy between a man and a woman, yet this closeness should not diminish but strengthen the individuality of each partner. A marriage that lasts is one that always has a little more to grow. It is out of the resonance between individuality and union that love, whose incredible strength is equal only to its incredible fragility, is born and reborn.

Marriage is a lifetime commitment, which recognizes the negative as well as the positive aspects of life. Marriage's content is never predetermined. It is a living organism that reflects the continuous choices of the individuals involved. In marrying we promise to love not only as we feel right now, but also as we intend to feel. In marriage we say not only, "I love you today," but also, "I promise to love you tomorrow, the next day and always."

Love doesn't limit. Love brings with it the gift of freedom. Love teaches us to encourage the people we love to make their own choices, seek their own path and learn their lessons in their own way and in their own time. Love also teaches us to share our feelings and thoughts with each other about those choices. We can then make decisions openly and freely, through our love that allows both to grow. Love that restrains is not love. To restrain another in the name of love, doesn't create love, it creates restraint. Love means each person is free to follow his or her own heart. If we truly love, our choices will naturally and freely serve that love well. When we give freedom to another, we really give freedom to ourselves.

In promising always, we promise each other time. We promise to exercise our love, to stretch it large enough to embrace the unforeseen realities of the future. We promise to learn to love beyond the level of our instincts and inclinations, to love in hard times as well as when we are exhilarated by the pleasures of romance.

We change because of these promises. We shape ourselves according to them; we live in their midst and live differently because of them. We feel protected because of them. We try some things and resist trying others because, having promised, we feel secure—to see, to be, to love. We are protected; our hearts have come home.

When we are safe in marriage, we can risk. Because we know we are loved, we can step beyond our fears; because we have chosen, we can transcend our insecurities. We can make mistakes, knowing we will not be cast out; take missteps, knowing someone will be there to catch us. And because mistakes and missteps are the stuff of change, of expansion, in marriage we can expand to our fullest capacity.

So remember these things, as you go out into the world as a couple: that your love will have seasons, that your relationship is a progression, and that love will prevail. Remembering each other, holding each other in your hearts and your minds, will give you a marriage as deep in its joy, as your courtship has been in its magic.

Congratulations (*Person B's name*) and (*Person A's name*), the real fun has just begun.

Opening Wishes

Enfolded in joy, inhabited by hope, bathed in the infinite spectrum of love, may you always be infused with it and beautifully enlightened by it. May every desire you have for your love be fulfilled. May your vision clearly behold one another. May you hear each other most genuinely. And may you give of your endless generosity to nourish one another's hearts and sweetly keep the promises you make here today.

Declaration of Intent

(*Person B's name*) and (*Person A's name*), you have declared your intention to make this venture of faith and love, realizing that from this time forward your destinies will be woven of one design and your challenges and joys will be shared together. Today you are making public, before family and friends, that the words, "I love you," are a full commitment of yourselves, one to the other.

Understanding that marriage is the convergence of your individual and joint destinies as well as the greatest support for them,

(*Person A's name*), do you choose to marry, (*Person B's name*) and have (him/her) as your (husband/wife).

> *Response:* I do

(*Person B's name*), do you choose to marry, (*Person A's name*) and have (her/him) as your (wife/husband).

> *Response:* I do

Vows

(Person B's name), Repeat after me:

> I choose you, (*Person A's name*),
> To be my (husband/wife), from this time forward.
> To love you, and be faithful to you,
> To be a comfort, in your life,
> To nourish you, with my gentleness,
> To uphold you, with my strength,
> To love your body, as it ages,
> To weigh the effects, of the words I speak
> And of the things I do,
> To never take you for granted,
> But always give thanks, for your presence.
> I promise you this, from my heart,
> For all the days of my life.

(Person A's name), Repeat after me:
> I choose you, (*Person B's name*),
> To be my (wife/husband), from this time forward.
> To love you, and be faithful to you,
> To be a comfort, in your life,
> To nourish you, with my gentleness,
> To uphold you, with my strength,
> To love your body, as it ages,
> To weigh the effects, of the words I speak
> And of the things I do,
> To never take you for granted,
> But always give thanks, for your presence.
> I promise you this, from my heart,
> For all the days of my life.

Ring Wishes

Rings are made precious by our wearing them. The rings you exchange at your wedding are the most special because they say that even in your uniqueness you have chosen to share your lives, to allow the presence of another human being to enhance who you are. As you wear them through time, they will reflect not only who you are, but also what you have created together.

Exchange of Rings

(Person A's name), Repeat after me:

> I give you this ring, as a symbol of my love
> And as a constant reminder

That I have chosen you, above all others
To be the one, to share my life.

(Person B's name), Repeat after me:

I give you this ring, as a symbol of my love
And as a constant reminder
That I have chosen you, above all others
To be the one, to share my life.

Pronouncement of Marriage

(*Person B's name*) and (*Person A's name*), because you have pledged your love and commitment to each other before these witnesses, I declare that you are (husband and wife/married). May the love that lives in and around all of us fill your hearts and infuse your lives.

The Kiss

You may now kiss to seal this union.

Closing Wishes

May you be supported, every step of your path. May you endlessly delight one another. May you rest in the comfort of knowing that you have chosen through one another to serve the highest purposes of love. Depart in peace, recognizing that what you undertake together will bring you infinite joy.

Presentation

It is my pleasure to introduce to you, (*Person B's name*) and (*Person A's name*), (last name), (husband and wife/married).

ZEN Ceremony

Welcome/Introduction

We have come together for the marriage of (*Person A's name*) and (*Person B's name*).

Address

Marriage begins in the giving of words. We cannot join ourselves to one another without giving our word. And this must be an unconditional giving, for in joining ourselves to one another we join ourselves to the unknown.

(*Person A's name*) and (*Person B's name*), you are about to take a new step forward into life. This day is made possible not only because of your love for each other, but through the grace of your parents and all of humanity.

Courtesy and consideration, even in anger and adversity, are the seeds of compassion. Love is the fruit of compassion. Trust, love, and respect are the sustaining virtues of marriage. They enable us to learn from each situation, and help us to realize that everywhere we turn we meet our Self.

We nourish ourselves and each other in living by the following five precepts:

1. We allow the fullest expression of our deepest Self.
2. We take full responsibility for our own life, in all its infinite dimensions.

3. We affirm our trust in the honesty and wisdom of our soul, which with our love and reverence always shows us the true way.

4. We are committed to embrace all parts of our Self, including our deepest fears and shadows, so that they may be transformed into light.

5. We affirm our willingness to keep our hearts open, even in the midst of great pain.

Dedication Blessing

May your fulfillment and joy in each other and in yourselves increase with every passing year. And, may you continue to deepen your life with each other and with all conscious beings.

Reading 1

And now (*Friend's name*) will read a selection chosen by (*Person B's name*) and (*Person A's name*).

(*A special selection of your choice.*)

Vows

Now (*Person B's name*) and (*Person A's name*) will exchange their marriage vows.

(*Person A's name*), *Repeat after me*

I, (*Person A's name*), take you, (*Person B's name*) to be my wife/husband, in equal love, as a mirror for my true Self, as a partner on my path, to honor and to cherish, in sorrow and in joy, till death do us part.

(*Person B's name*), *Repeat after me*

> I, (*Person B's name*), take you, (*Person A's name*) to be my
> husband/wife, in equal love, as a mirror for my true Self, as
> a partner on my path, to honor and to cherish, in sorrow
> and in joy, till death do us part.

Reading 2

And now (*Friend's name*) will read a selection chosen by (*Person B's
name*) and (*Person A's name*).

> (*A special selection of your choice.*)

Ring Exchange

Now (*Person B's name*) and (*Person A's name*) celebrate their love
and proclaim their union with rings of precious metal. The
precious nature of their rings represents the subtle and wonderful
essence they find individually, through their mutual love, respect,
and support. The metal itself represents the long life they may
cultivate together, not only in years, but in all the infinite dimensions of each moment they share.

You may now exchange rings.

> [*Couple exchanges rings*]

Because of your choice to share a life and the vows made here
today, I pronounce you, (husband and wife/married).

You may kiss to seal this vow.

Celtic Ceremony

Celtic Wedding History

There were many rituals associated with wedding ceremonies among Celtic peoples. The most important aspect of all Celtic weddings was the feast. This included the families of the bride and groom as well as friends and members of the community. Unlike weddings today, which separate the wedding ceremony and the reception, Celts viewed the whole affair as one grand ceremony. The community was there to solidify the bond between the Bride and Groom. The Celtic bride was held in great esteem. The term "Bride" is Celtic in origin, coming from Brigid, the goddess and saint of Celtic lore.

Celtic weddings were simple and meaningful. They often took place outside in nature to bless the union. Nature was very important to the Celts. They believed the soul existed within and outside of an individual. The soul would manifest in the trees, the rocks, the waters and the sun. Humans and the world around them were intertwined, the soul connected to the spirit of the earth. Their belief in marriage was that two souls would join together so their strengths would be twice as great and hardships only half as difficult.

The ceremony itself was a very simple ritual called handfasting. The bride and groom would stand facing each other holding hands and they were bound by a ceremonial rope, cord, or wrap. This is where the term "tying the knot" comes from. This symbolically signified the unity of the couple. To finalize the marriage the couple would hold hands and jump over a branch or a broom into their new life together.

Celtic Ceremony #1

[If the ceremony takes place outdoors, trees, water and other natural elements provide an inspiring setting. If the ceremony takes place indoors, green branches from an oak tree, branches from an evergreen during winter months, and flowers will provide the proper spirit. An altar should be prepared which contains incense, three candles, a two foot length of silk rope, a chalice or cup and a pitcher filled with wine or ale and an oak branch (two feet in length is sufficient). The incense should be lit before the start of the ceremony.]

Welcome/Introduction

Friends, family and members of the community, welcome to this ceremony, which will unite two souls in marriage.

Address

Marriage is an agreement, which should not be entered into lightly. It is the union of two souls, two hearts and two minds. The Celtic concept of the soul encompasses far more than we traditionally think of today. The Celtic belief of the soul exists within and outside the individual; it is manifest in the trees, the rocks, the waters and the Sun. The relationship between humanity and the world around them is intertwined. The soul is inextricably tied to the Universal spirit of the Earth.

Celtic Trinity Ceremony

The Celtic trinity is an ancient profession of faith that maintains that trust in the soul, belief in the heart and faith in the mind, are all that is needed to lead an honorable, loving and fulfilled life.

(*Person B's name*) and (*Person A's name*), in marriage, your souls will join together so that your strengths shall be twice as great and your hardships will be only half as difficult.

As you share the (ale/wine) from this wedding cup let it remind you to trust in your soul which is the Universal spirit. Trust in its strength and it will strengthen the bond between you.

[Officiant pours the wine or ale into the cup and hands it to Person A, who takes a sip and hands it to Person B, who takes a sip, and hands it back to the Officiant.]

[Officiant then holds up the silk rope.]

Please place your hands over one another.

Your open hands placed over one another represent your hearts. The silk rope represents the belief, which binds them together.

Belief in your heart is a testament to the power of love and compassion. Belief in your heart is the constant desire to put your spouse before you in every way, to act mindful and to allow love and patience to prevail. Belief in your heart will always guide your marriage and allow the power of love to grow, multiply and strengthen. At times, your souls may drift apart, but the belief in your heart will act as a silk tether, which will keep you together.

[Officiant then binds together their hands by wrapping the silk rope around them.]

Having faith in your mind is the last concept of the Celtic trinity. May each of you maintain your independence of mind, respecting each others thoughts and trying to learn from one another. May positive thoughts always guide you.

[Officiant lights the candles]

These candles represent the light that burns away the darkness of ignorance. May you always strive to keep your mind bright, sharp and uncluttered. Your mindfulness will add joy and ease to your marriage.

Vows

(*Person A's name*), *Repeat after me*

> I, (*Person A's name*), take (*Person B's name*), as my (wife/husband) and vow to be mindful in our journey together, to love (her/him) and to cherish (her/him), to trust in the Universal soul, to have belief in my heart and faith in my mind. From this day forward our souls will be as one.

(*Person B's name*), *Repeat after me*

> I, (*Person B's name*), take (*Person A's name*), as my (husband/wife) and vow to be mindful in our journey together, to love (him/her) and cherish (him/her) to trust in the Universal soul, to have belief in my heart and faith in my mind. From this day forward our souls will be as one.

Jumping the Branch

[Officiant holds up the branch.]

It is tradition to jump over a branch together to finalize the marriage. This symbolizes the transition into a new existence where you are committed to each other and to a life of growth and love.

[Officiant places the branch on the ground]

(*Person B's name*) and (*Person A's name*), please join hands now and jump over the branch into your new life together.

[The couple jumps over the branch.]

Pronouncement

By the power vested in me by the State of (*State's Name*), I now declare you to be (husband and wife/married).

The Kiss

You may kiss to seal this union.

Making It Legal

Who Can Perform Your Ceremony?

Most states in the US recognize licensed or ordained ministers, officiants, clergymen, priests, rabbis, pastors, judges and justices of the peace as authorized to perform marriage ceremonies. In some states government officials may be authorized to legally perform the ceremony. Contrary to some popular beliefs, no State currently authorizes ship captains to perform marriages.

Each State has its own criteria for who can legally perform a marriage ceremony. The following reference is a website that lists the criteria by State, but it is still recommended that you confirm with the County Clerk in the state where the wedding will take place to verify the current requirements.

Criteria by State:
http://marriage.about.com/cs/marriagelicenses/a/officiants.htm

If you know someone whom you would like to perform the ceremony, and they are not currently ordained, there are organizations that ordain ministers either online or through the mail (see the "How to Become Ordained" section of this book).

How to Become Ordained

Becoming an Officiant

An Officiant is someone who performs a religious rite or presides over a religious service or ceremony. It is simply another word for Clergy or Minister and commonly used to refer to people authorized to perform marriage ceremonies, especially for non-denominational and non-religious ceremonies.

The United States in general does not attempt to define what an organization must be in order to qualify as a Church or what qualifications are necessary to be a minister. This goes back to early American history and the separation of Church and State. Each religious denomination has its own requirements for becoming ordained.

If you wish to become ordained and are not affiliated with a particular religious denomination, there are several religious organizations in the US that provide non-denominational ordination (no training necessary, sometimes a fee is charged). One of these organizations is Universal Life Church. By visiting their website and completing a form online, a person can become ordained for free with the click of a button and yes (as of this writing) it is legal in all 50 states.

Website for Universal Life Church: http://www.themonastery.org/

Some States require you to either register a Letter of Good Standing or a Copy of your credentials at the County Court house. Other States require you to request and file an application. It is recommended that you verify the requirements for the state where the ceremony will take place with the County Clerk prior to performing a marriage ceremony.

For information on Officiant requirements by state:
http://usmarriagelaws.com/

Considerations When Selecting an Officiant

It is important to choose the Officiant (also known as 'Minister') who best demonstrates the ability to carry out your desires. The words spoken at your ceremony should reflect what the two of you believe and feel. Here are some tips on what to consider when selecting an Officiant.

What is the Officiant's experience?

The government does not issue licenses to ministers, so an Officiant's experience with weddings is important. How many has he or she performed? Does the Officiant have references you can contact? Does the Officiant have credentials he or she can show you?

What is the spiritual or religious perspective of the Officiant?

Many ministers subscribe to the doctrines of a particular faith. If you are not of the same faith, let him or her know what your religious values are in the first meeting. Can they work with you to create a ceremony that is true to *your* beliefs, or do you feel that the Officiant has an agenda to conform your ceremony into his or her particular denominational preferences? Will he or she work well with your beliefs?

How accommodating is the Officiant?

If you want a non-traditional song played during the ceremony, will the Officiant allow it? Are you free to add your own vows or other special, romantic touches? Do you want a little humor in the ceremony? Even if you don't know what kind of wedding ceremony you want, are you confident that the Officiant will allow for changes as the wedding day approaches? Will the Officiant allow flash photography during the wedding? Will the Officiant work with you to develop a ceremony, which honors your religious or non-religious traditions and beliefs?

What moral criteria does the Officiant expect you to meet?

If you and your fiancé are living together, already have children, are expecting a child, or if either of you have been through a divorce, it is important to tell the prospective Officiant your situation during your first phone conversation. Some Officiants will reject you immediately, or express other expectations and it is better to find this out early.

What about premarital counseling?

Some couples want counseling, and others do not feel it is necessary. Some Officiants offer excellent counseling programs, but others may pressure you into "counseling" programs that ask you to sign a tithing agreement or make a commitment to join a particular church and attend faithfully every week. Counseling programs offered by an Officiant as well as those offered independently, are only as good as your willingness to deeply participate. Some people definitely benefit from them, but many do not, especially if you are simply fulfilling an obligation by attending the sessions. The decision is yours, and the Officiant you select should respect and honor that decision.

How many meetings will you have?

Some Officiants say no meeting is necessary, that he or she will just show up for the wedding and you can run your own rehearsal. Others want you to go through their extensive premarital counseling. Some will offer one or two preparatory meetings and a rehearsal. Some are unwilling to meet with you in person if you are just "shopping around." What do you want? Can the Officiant meet your wishes? Will the Officiant be available to talk by phone as questions arise? What is your preferred method of working with them to create your ceremony? Are they willing to meet in person, or do they only work with you over the phone or via email?

Will the Officiant run the rehearsal?

An experienced Officiant at your wedding rehearsal can be very helpful, but he or she may not be available at the scheduled time. If the Officiant is unable or unwilling to attend the rehearsal, will other arrangements be made for someone to lead your wedding party through the steps? For more elaborate weddings, it is important to have someone available to guide you and your attendees through the practice of your ceremony, so that you know what to expect. Also, ask the Officiant if it is okay for the two of you to face one another during the ceremony (your guests will be able to see your faces instead of your backs).

What will the Officiant wear?

Some Officiants wear suits (a black suit is desirable as it blends in with any color scheme), some wear robes, and others wear a wide variety of garments from jeans and tennis shoes to butterfly wings (yes, someone actually showed up to perform a ceremony wearing butterfly wings)! Ask to see a picture of the clothing that will be worn on your wedding day, to determine if it looks suitable. If it is too ornate, or if it has prominent religious symbols which may offend some family members, ask the Officiant if he or she would consider wearing a basic suit instead.

What ceremony choices does the Officiant offer?

Many officiants have only one ceremony they offer. Be sure you get to review their ceremony and ensure that it expresses what you want communicated at your wedding. Ask if they have any spontaneous words they will add. Some Officiants will have a few simple choices (with the option of adding some of your own ideas) so that you can create the ceremony that is the most mean-ingful to you. Others will design an elaborate, customized wedding just for you.

Ask how long they think the ceremony itself will take; this is important information for your facility, photographer, caterer, etc. You may prefer something simpler than what the Officiant is offering, or more flexible. Whatever you want, let the Officiant know in advance.

Is the Officiant focused on serving you?

Many people feel that they have to meet a minister's (also known as 'Officiant') standards, and in some religious traditions this is entirely valid. But remember, the original meaning of the word "minister" is "servant." Is the minister serving your needs on your big day? Are you comfortable in their presence, or do you feel like you have to withhold things to prevent his or her disapproval? Do you feel pressured to behave differently to gain their approval? Find an Officiant who is eager to serve you, and your wedding day will be a beautiful one for everyone.

Obtaining the Marriage License

What is the difference between the Marriage License and the Marriage Certificate? The marriage *license* is a legal document, obtained by the couple, that authorizes a designated party to perform the ceremony, allowing you to get married; and the marriage *certificate* is the form filed with the State which officially certifies that the nuptials took place and once recorded is the official document that proves you are married (a certified copy may be requested from the State once the marriage has been recorded).

To determine the location and requirements to obtain a marriage license, contact the local marriage license county or city clerk office in the state where the marriage will take place.

For information on how to obtain your marriage license by state and county: http://usmarriagelaws.com/

Marriage License Laws in the US

Each State has specific Marriage License laws for a couple to wed. Although there are differences between the requirements in the various states, a marriage performed in one state must be recognized by every other state under the Full Faith and Credit Clause of the United States Constitution.

The following reference is a website that lists the criteria by State, but it is still recommended that you confirm with the state where the wedding will take place to verify the current requirements.

For information on Marriage License Laws by State:
http://usmarriagelaws.com/

Filing the Paperwork

The couple receives the appropriate documents when they apply for their Marriage License. The couple then provides the Officiant with the Marriage License and Marriage Certificate documents prior to the wedding ceremony. A portion of the Marriage Certificate form will be completed by the couple in advance of the ceremony and the rest of it will be completed after the ceremony (i.e. signing the document and Officiant information).

After the marriage ceremony is performed, the Officiant (or person who performs the marriage ceremony) has a duty to send a copy of the Marriage Certificate to the county or state agency that records marriage certificates. The couple may then request a certified copy of the certificate from the county or state agency once the marriage has been recorded. Some Officiants will order a certified copy for the couple as an added service at the time they send in the paperwork.

Failure to send the marriage certificate to the appropriate agency does not necessarily nullify the marriage, but it may make proof of the marriage more difficult.

Bibliography

Kingma, Daphne Rose. Weddings from the Heart: Ceremonies for an Unforgettable Wedding. Berkeley, CA: Conari, 1991. Print.

About the Author

Dayna Reid, Bestselling Author, Writer, and Minister. She has officiated weddings for over 14 years. Her love for people and the desire to provide couples with a non-judgmental and personalized approach to selecting the words spoken at their wedding inspired her to seek ministry ordination. Although Dayna personally believes in God, she also believes, "Everyone has to find their own way in this world, including any beliefs they may have about the mysteries. Because truly, all we really have is a faith in what we believe to be true."

Officiant/Minister Coaching and Consulting

Dayna Reid has officiated weddings for over 14 years and provided consulting to many newly ordained officiants/ministers who want to perform wedding ceremonies and want to offer personalized services to their clients. She has also coached several established ministers in how to transition their wedding ministry into a business.

For a 15-minute, complementary consultation, contact:
www.Marriage-Vows.com

Sacred Ceremony

Create and Officiate Personalized Wedding Ceremonies

Dayna Reid's bestselling book includes: Step-by-step, informative chapters, which describe the elements of a wedding ceremony from beginning to end, and the choices people can make with each element. "*Sacred Ceremony*" includes a wealth of wording and ceremony selections, to celebrate diverse styles, beliefs and traditions, from Christian to Zen, to the simple declarations of love that transcend tradition.

Do-It-Yourself Wedding Ceremony

Choosing the Perfect Words and Officiating Your Unforgettable Day

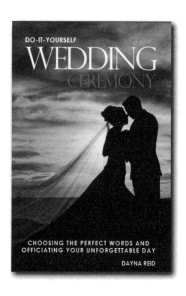

Dayna Reid's revised edition of the book previously titled, "*Sacred Ceremony*," includes: Step-by-step, informative chapters, which describe the elements of a wedding ceremony from beginning to end, and the choices people can make with each element. "*Do-It-Yourself Wedding Ceremony*" includes a wealth of wording and ceremony selections, to celebrate diverse styles, beliefs and traditions, from Christian to Zen, to the simple declarations of love that transcend tradition.